P9-DEL-411

PIGS ON THE FARM

Cliff Moon

Illustrated by Anna Jupp

A DOWN ON THE FARM BOOK

THE BOOKWRIGHT PRESS
NEW YORK · 1983

Other books in this series

DAIRY COWS ON THE FARM
SHEEP ON THE FARM
POULTRY ON THE FARM

Published in the United States in 1983 by
The Bookwright Press, 387 Park Avenue South, New York NY 10016.
First published in 1983 by
Wayland Publishers Ltd, England.
© Copyright 1983 Wayland Publishers Ltd

ISBN: 0-531-04696-6
Library of Congress Catalog Card Number: 83-71630
Printed in Italy by
G. Canale & C.S.p.A., Turin

636.4
m

Contents

132330

Look at the picture.

The family is ready for breakfast.

They are having eggs, french fries, bacon and sausages.

Bacon and sausages come from pigs, and this book is about pigs.

5

The family is visiting a pig farm.
At first they can only see
the big *boars* in their pens.
Boars are male pigs.
All the other pigs are indoors.

Here are three *sows* eating vegetables.
Sows are female pigs.
They will soon have piglets, so
they need to walk around outside
to get exercise.
There is an electric wire across the field.
What do you think it is for?

(Answer on page 32)

9

The piglets have been born, and
they are drinking the sow's milk.
Sows often have ten piglets, but
sometimes they have more.
Once a sow had 34 piglets!

Now the piglets are about five weeks old,
and they are eating on their own.
The sows are chained up so that
they will not go far away.
But the piglets can wander around.
They shelter in the little sheds
at night or when it rains.

In winter the sow and her piglets
live indoors in a pen, or *sty*.
Piglets have to keep warm, so the farmer
has hung a heater over their pen.

15

These pigs are getting fat.
They stay in their pens, and
the farmer feeds them.
They must eat and eat to get
fatter and fatter.

Every week the farmer weighs his pigs.
He can sell them only
when they are just the right weight.
Meat from pigs is called pork.
Bacon and ham are two other kinds of
meat we get from pigs.
Pigs sold for bacon must be heavier
than pigs sold for ham.

These pigs are ready to be sold.
They will go to market in a truck.
Some of them are too small to sell for
meat, so another farmer will buy them
and fatten them.
Some pigs get too heavy.
What do you think happens to them?
(Answer on page 32)

The pigs have been butchered.
They did not feel any pain
when they were killed.
These men are cutting up the meat
with electric saws.

Now the meat is in a butcher's shop.
It all looks different, but
it all came from pigs.
There are pies, sausages, chops,
slices of bacon and
large pieces of pork and ham.
Pigs are useful for other things
which you cannot eat.
Can you think what they are?
(Answer on page 32)

This pig has been killed on the farm
for the farmer's family to eat.
The farmer sent for a butcher.
The butcher knew how to kill the pig
so that it would not feel any pain.
Now they will set fire to the straw
to burn the bristles off the pig's skin.
Why do you think the woman has a bowl?

(Answer on page 32)

Now the farmer can make different things
from the pig.
These people are making bacon
from the back and sides of the pig.
Can you see the hams hanging up
behind them?

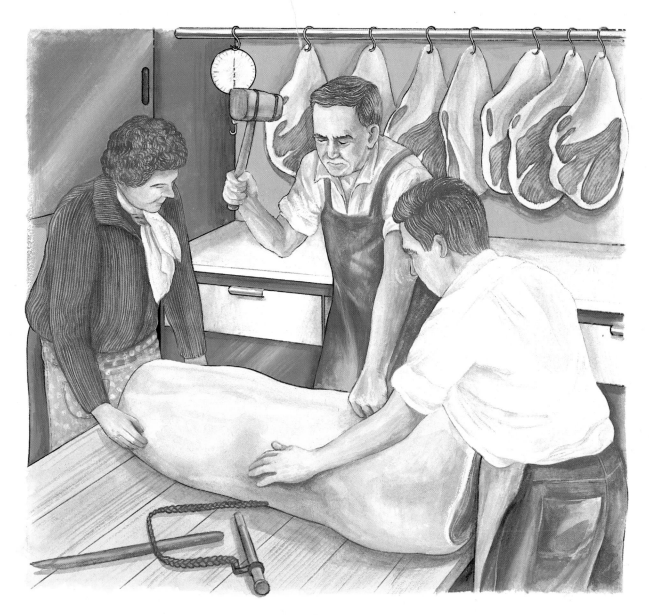

Here are seven different kinds of pigs.
Middle White pigs make good roast pork and ham.
Large White pigs are all good for roasts,
ham and bacon.
The other five are all good for bacon.
Do you like bacon?

Large White

Middle White

Landrace

Gloucester
Old Spot

Hampshire

Large Black

Tamworth

Unit District #5 Elementary
Instructional Media Center

31

Answers to questions

Page 8
The electric wire gives a small shock when touched, and stops the pigs straying past it.

Page 20
Pigs that are too heavy are killed
and made into sausages.

Page 24
You can make *leather* from a pig's skin and *brushes* from a pig's bristles.

Page 26
The woman has a bowl to catch the pig's blood.
She will use it to make a sausage called
blood sausage.

Index

Unit
Instructional Media Center